MW01612982

BLESSINGS IN BROKEN PLACES

From Abandonment to Abundance

by

Mel Jackson

BLESSINGS IN BROKEN PLACES

From Abandonment to Abundance

by

Mel Jackson

Copyright 2021 ICHAMPION Publishing

All right reserved. No portion of this book may be reproduced, scanned, stored in a retrieval system, transmitted in any form or by any means- electronically, mechanically, photocopy, recording or any other- except for brief quotations in printed reviews, without written permission of the publisher. Please do not participate or encourage piracy or copyrighted materials in violation of the author's rights. Purchase only authorized editions.

Published by iCHAMPION Publishing

P.O. Box 2352 Frisco, TX 75034

Content edit by Nikia Hammonds-Blakely and iCHAMPION Publishing

Library of Congress Cataloging-in-Publication Data Publisher and Printing by iCHAMPION Publishing

Written By: Mel Jackson
Cover Design By: iCHAMPION Publishing
Contributing Illustrator: Gerard Claiborne

ISBN: 978-1-7367112-4-8

Self-Help

Personal Development

Dear God,

Thank you for pressing me, shaping me, and molding me. Thank you for allowing my experiences to stretch me and allowing me to grow through them. Thank you for showing me the essence of beauty for ashes. The healing that I have received throughout this process has been refreshing and, at times, overwhelming. I have learned things about myself that I could have never even imagined. I became one with my broken places. I learned that the gift of acceptance is one of the best gifts ever known to man. Yet, the gift of surrendering soothes and feeds the spirit like no other. This experience has been nothing short of amazing, a true honor and privilege to sit at your feet and commune with you in a way I never have before. You've gracefully broken me. You pushed me to the bare limits of the place from which greatness is birthed and showed me how to live in the moment.

I dedicate this book to my grandmother, Hazel Marie Benjamin, my inspiration and my best friend.

You are the flower that blooms in the springtime.
You are my heartbeat and the stars that shine.
You are my biggest supporter and my rock.
You held me up and pushed me when I wanted to stop.
You are the essence of strength in my eyes,
You are the joy and the smile forever by my side.
I Love you! Forever (BayBay)

Sunrise March 27, 1940 - Sunset March 3, 2020

ACKNOWLEDGEMENTS

To My Daughter Zatavia - You will forever be my angel in the sky. Losing you was the ultimate testament of God's grace and mercy.

To My Goddaughter Kaylee - You're a living, breathing reflection of God's heart for me when he took my own. Born the next day, you gave me hope.

To My Mother - No matter what happens in life, I'm grateful to God for picking you for me. I love you with all of me.

To My Dad Michael Jackson - Thanks for never judging me and always being receptive to my pure emotions.

To My Dad John Jr. - Thank you for loving, nurturing, and caring for me.

To My God-Mom Jerrie Elaire - Thank you for taking me under your wing, leading and guiding me daily, loving me unconditionally, and refusing to see me settle for less than who I was called to be. The gift of your love will never go unnoticed.

To My Little Sister - Being your role model means the world. I am grateful to God daily for gracing me with your love.

To My Niece Harmoni - You are my little best friend. Your love for me is as pure as the sunshine.

To My Nephew Keith - In your eyes, I am the best auntie in the world.

To Carolyn Sanders "Mommy" - Thank you for continuously reminding me of the gifts that are locked up in me, constantly praying over me, allowing God to use you to accomplish His will in my life, and loving me as though I am your own.

To My Cousin Linda - You are the best big sister cousin a girl could ever have. You and Gerard celebrate me daily just for being me. For that, I love you both unfailing.

To My Cousin Essie - You are the true definition of style and grace.

To Tracy – Thank you for praying for me even when your life was falling apart. Thank you for selflessly building me up and at times putting the call on my life before your own.

To Auntie Scoodie - Thank you for always covering and protecting me.

To Mrs. Sherri - Thank you for gracefully caring for me daily.

To Deiondra - The grace of our relationship taught me that even coming from two different backgrounds, we all hurt, and we all love.

To Khaliah - Thank you for always being there on call day and night to help me.

To Maya - At my lowest points you pray and encourage me.

To Pam - You've been my best friend of thirty plus years. We have been through so much together. This friendship is a gift that will never end.

To Teresa J - My therapist, you work through the rough patches with me daily, yet you always remind me of the beauty that lies beneath the surface. You have been consistent in helping me change my perception and refocus on what is to come.

To Stephani Marshall-Ross - Thanks for believing in my gift and pushing me, for always finding a way, for accepting the role of the front line of my life, and for caring for and protecting my brand as though it is your own.

To Nikia Hammonds – Thank you for allowing God to lead you, for being obedient to the call of God in your life, and for agreeing to take me by the hand to birth this thing. You gave me your word that you would be the midwife that God used to deliver this baby in this season. Know my gratitude is never failing.

To all my family and friends that have lent me their ears, listening to bits and pieces of my heart as I poured out what has been locked inside of me for years - Thank you for always giving me your honest opinions and nothing shy of your love and support.

~Mel

Sunrise December 31, 1974 - Sunset June 8, 2019

Maria – Losing you was the ultimate test of love and pain.
It taught me resilience on a new level.
It grew me and nurtured me.

CONTENTS

INTRODUCTION

We all have been broken at some point in our lives. I believe some have been broken a few times by one thing or another.

Do not become discouraged while trying to accept the pain of your past, put passion into the things you love, praying for peace, and becoming sure of your purpose.

Life has a way of forcing us to shift, move, change direction and reevaluate everything and everyone around us. At least that has been my experience. There have been times I thought I knew it all. I thought I had mastered the art of the very things that held me back—pushing my way past every hurt, every door that had slammed in my face, and every person that I believed betrayed me. I tried finding answers to the very things that haunted me night after night as I lay in my bed thinking, often with eyes full of tears that felt like the sun shining on a warm summer day as they rolled down my cheeks.

I began writing this book in 2012. At that point, I had been broken, abused, abandoned, and healed enough, so I thought. I began thinking I could use my experiences to help someone else. At times, I would feel like there was so much more that I would experience, things that would make my story even more helpful to those that would lend me their ears long enough to listen. Those who would be bold enough to put themselves in my shoes as I began telling a story would remind them of their very own truths and wanted to heal and do so correctly.

The stories of my life are things that have been fueled with every distraction you could ever imagine. Some of which brought me to tears at every thought of them, crying because they hurt, and rejoicing because I lived through them. Many of which I walked through alone. I understand that, although often a lonely place, it was the only way it would ever build true character and self-respect. It was the only way I would ever see the beauty that radiated within me and stared back at me when I looked in the mirror. It would become the mere art and essence of how I would learn to love myself and how I would push myself. It would become the only way I could ever truly live the life I dreamed of and reach the highest peaks of my intelligence.

Daily life hands us lessons on life, love, power, and most of all, truth. A truth that no one wants to hear and realities no one wants to face. We can find ourselves caught between what is real and what we believe to be real.

My Vision

To live my life physically and mentally fulfilling.

That I may be an example to those around me.

Remaining **Loyal**, **Dependable**, and **Loving** to

Myself and Others

So that the Beautiful Soul beneath the surface

May be a true reflection of what those whom I encounter

See outwardly!!!!

— Mel J.

Distraction 1:

ABUSE

"When the purpose is not known, abuse is inevitable."
— Myles Monroe

"Don't judge yourself by what others did to you."
— C. Kennedy, Ómorphi

I grew up in a small town near Beaumont, Texas, called Woodville. I am sure you can tell by the name that this is not the best place for opportunities and advancement. It was a tranquil country town with miles of trees and a substantial amount of dirt roads.

In the summer, I loved the smell of the flowers and the freshly bloomed berries. There was a field down the street from my grandmother that had thousands of berry bushes. My friends and I would often go walking down there and pick berries that our grandmothers would later use to make blackberry pies. Boy, were they good! You had to catch them warm and fresh out of the oven. That was when they were at their best.

My grandmother raised me; my mom was 17 when she had me. My parents were never married, and to tell you the truth, I never really had a relationship with my father until I was 13. I visited him a few times as a child and often saw him around because we lived in the same town.

If you're wondering if I ever wanted to have a closer relationship with him as a kid, well, the truth of the matter is that I never really thought about it. I was my mom's only child and my grandmother's only grandchild at the time, not to mention that my aunt and uncle had no kids of their own as I was coming up either, so I never really wanted for a whole lot. I guess you could say I was spoiled.

We did not have a lot of money, but I never went without anything. My mother was married to her first husband, whom I knew as my father during the early part of my childhood, and he also took excellent care of me. I remember the day they got married in my grandmother's yard. That's how they did things back where I am from – when I was coming up.

I will never forget that day. I had on the cutest little white dress with my ruffled socks and white patent leather shoes. I was the flower girl. Still, he has been more than a father to me even after the divorce.

My mother later remarried, and who would have known that the choice she made that day would write the final chapter in how our relationship would turn out? Things were okay between them in the beginning, I guess. I really can't say because I never lived with her. When she decided to move in with him, I stayed with my grandmother and would visit her periodically on the weekends, but that did not often happen because my mother worked a lot.

I will never forget the summer that I stayed with her. Some friends and I went swimming, and when I returned, my mother was not home. I was nervous because of the way her husband always looked at me. Imagine being nine years old and having a man look at you as though you were the best pick of ribs in the meat cooler. That is an uncomfortable situation to be in, not to mention scary. To top it off, this day, he tried coming into the bathroom with me to help me take a shower.

I was nine, and I did not need any help at this age. My mother never even attempted to help me bathe. I was perfectly capable of doing it on my own. I was so terrified that I took my shower with my swimsuit still on, and no child should have to experience such humiliation.

I wanted to tell my mother time and time again, and I often hinted around it on numerous occasions. I always felt that if she confronted him, he would hit her and make her fear him more than she already did. She had been through so much mental and physical abuse in her marriage and I was afraid of what would happen to her. I have replayed countless events in my mind that gave me reason to question her safety. One in particular when I was seven years old, I will never forget her leaving him and moving in with my grandmother and me. One day, he came over and insisted on seeing her. Well, she decided that she would go to the door and talk with him. He planned to get her to move back in with him, but she was unwilling to do so. I remember hearing this scream, and I ran to see what in the world was going on.

It was summertime, and earlier that day, I had been out swimming in an inflatable swimming pool that they would blow up to fill with water and set on the side of the house. That is what I swam in because we couldn't afford a real pool. When they brought my pool in, it was left in the hallway by the front door. By the time I made it to the door where my mom was, her mouth was bleeding. My pool was completely covered in blood, and he was nowhere in sight. Because of that, at an early age, I feared for her life.

It is devastating for a child to see your mother being abused, and there is nothing you can do to help her.

When I look back, now as an adult, I know that not telling my mother about the passes he made at me was a mistake because it just continued to happen. My mother had decided to try and make her marriage work and moved back in with him. He went from trying to help me shower to offering me money to fulfill his sick fantasies.

My cousin would often come to visit with us during the summer. One particular summer, she stayed at my mothers' house. She was older than me, but we were close, so I decided to go and spend some time with her. I felt as though there was not a lot he could do because she would share my room. I was wrong again. My cousin, Mo, decided to stay the night with her friend who lived two houses down the street. I cried to go with her, but my mother said no. They were very strict during my childhood, and I seldom was allowed to spend the night with friends. While she lay sound asleep in her bed, he flashed money at me and suggested that if I did something for him, he would persuade my mother to let me go. I started screaming loud enough to wake her and used being afraid of the dark as an excuse. It's heartbreaking to know a person can be so sick-minded to the point where they put a child in a position to feel as though they have to keep their being mistreated bottled up because of fear and guilt. Though he never physically touched me, the mental abuse, looks, and random gestures made were mentally damaging. As much as we hate to hear it, this is something that happens every day.

For me, being with my grandmother was a safe place, a place of peace as a kid, and that's where I loved to be. My grandmother worked as a home health aide for years. I remember going to work with her during the summer and helping her with her patients. Daily, we would go from house to house together, checking up on them. I must admit, I loved every bit of it, and she enjoyed having me there.

One day, the joy that I once knew was disrupted when my mother came and demanded that I relocate with her. She had moved to the DFW metroplex Dallas area three months prior. I did not want to go, but I had no choice. My grandmother was not too thrilled with the idea, but what was she to do? After all, it was my mother. So we said our goodbyes, and that was that. I would call her every day just to have some sense of remembrance of the comfort zone I once knew. Talking to her was a familiar place for me, which helped me deal with my unfamiliar circumstances.

You see, there comes the point in our lives where we have to go back to what is familiar to cope with change. I honestly didn't know what I would do in a new place with people I didn't know. Being a country girl and moving to the city was a big adjustment for me. I would often get sick, from time to time, dealing with climate changes. Where I am from, it was very humid, and the city was oh, so different. It's so much like the move of God in our lives; going from one level to the next is never comfortable, but you have to adjust. You might kick and scream. Your clothes might be a little ragged from the constant battling, but once you feel your way through with faith as your backbone, it becomes normal.

I could not stand the way my step-father treated her. As I mentioned before, there were times where she would leave him, but he would harass her to the point where she would always go back. As they say, "Sometimes love makes people do the craziest things." So you can see why I hated the day she demanded that I move away with her *and him.*

I sat staring at my grandmother, praying that she could get her to change her mind, but it would not happen this time. Any other time in my life, she had always persuaded my mother in a certain direction if she felt it would be best for me but not that day.

That was the longest car ride of my life, moving to Dallas, so far away from my grandmother and the only life I had known. She had been my best friend and my protector. But, in my opinion, my mom couldn't even protect herself from the toxic marriage that she had become a victim to, so I questioned how she would protect me. I was scared and nervous all at the same time. I didn't know what to expect on the journey that awaited me, nor did I know when or if I would ever see my grandmother again.

So there I was in a new place meeting new people. With each passing day, it became easier. The home was good, and I had tons of family and cousins my age with whom I could spend time. They often came over to visit. At first, things seemed to be going well. There were no arguments, no fighting, and I remember thinking that maybe this wasn't all that bad after all.

I had made some new friends, and I was finally learning to adjust. They would often tease me because of how I spoke, as I had country slang. I have always been a good communicator; you can take the girl out of the country, but never the country out of the girl. Life was slowly unfolding.

I stayed out of my stepfather's way as often as I could. My thoughts were, "The less I am in his presence, the less chance there was for him to make me feel uncomfortable." I didn't want to cause any problems or draw any attention to myself.

I was growing up and becoming a young lady. If I had turned him on in my early stages, only God knew what he would try at this point. I stayed gone as often as I could. My mom, being strict, made it hard sometimes. She didn't trust me staying the night with anyone. I guess she feared that of any parent, you never know what's going on in someone's household, and you don't want to expose your child to anything that you can prevent. What she did not know is the very thing she tried to protect me from, I was suffering right under her nose.

Then it began. The fights started. I would be asleep in my bed sometimes and awaken to her screams. I remember covering my head with my pillow. I even remember times where I would sit under her all night and want to sleep in bed with her when he was gone. I just knew that would protect her if he came home in a bad mood. It got to the point where I would hear him come home, and I would go in the living room and talk with them—doing anything I could to try and gauge his mood.

If he was upset about something, I tried my hardest to make him happy because I just didn't want him hitting her. I disliked being in his presence because it creeped me out, but if I had to bear a conversation with him to keep my mom safe, that's what I did. I learned at an early age how to protect the people that I loved. The only problem was I didn't know who would protect me. It molded me into a person who would go through grave lengths to protect those I loved, even if it was from an unhealthy place—learning to cover up my emotions and frustration while smiling through the pain.

I would often be on punishment because I missed curfew, and I even ran away a few times. I guess you could say I rebelled because I did not want to be there. The more she tried to keep me home, the more I contested it. I had never been a problem child or fast, as they would say. I was always very respectful. In my efforts to run from the pain, I just acted out of character from time-to-time as any other child would. It was like being in a house of mirrors that tormented me at every turn. No matter what mirror I looked in, I hated what I saw. Finally, in one mirror, I saw shame, so I ran. Then hurt flashed at me. Trying to find my way through, I became consumed with all the things I tried to escape. They horrified me.

Was this all my life was meant to be? Would I ever experience the beauty of healthy emotions separate from the pain? Would I ever be free? I wanted desperately to be free. I wanted to believe that freedom would soon find me. The thought of it was captivating. I longed for it. To some degree, maybe, it would appease the pain. It would become a bandage over it that would hide the scars, or perhaps it would give me the truth, a revelation or defining moment that would provide me with comfort. At least it might provide me comfort enough to live with what I had gone through daily.

Reflections

1. What do you consider to be abuse?

2. What abuse have you suffered in life?

3. How did you deal with the abuse you suffered?

4. How did it affect or define the path you took going forward?

5. If you have never suffered from any abuse, do you know someone who has?

6. Based on what you read in the previous chapter, how would you deal with abuse or help someone else deal?

7. Consider the scripture "Come to me, all you who are weary and burdened, and I will give you rest (Matthew 11:28). How do you relate it to the healing process of overcoming abuse?

_____

_____

_____

_____

_____

_____

_____

_____

_____

_____

_____

_____

_____

_____

_____

_____

_____

_____

Distraction 2:

ABANDONMENT

"The action or fact of abandoning or being abandoned."

"Stab the body, and it heals, but injure the heart,
and the wound lasts a lifetime."
— Mineko Iwasaki

Imagine being at the point in your life where you should be having fun, getting ready for senior trips, and loving life, only to have that disrupted and wake up to responsibilities that you have never known before. At 17, I was forced to grow up on my own and learn how to be a woman. I was in a position where I was making all the decisions for my life with no parental guidance. Could you even imagine experiencing life as a teenager and grown-up all at once? I was once asked the question, "If there was anything in my life that I could change, what would it be?" Honestly, it's the paths that we choose that make us who we are. You see, my mother decided to move back home to the country, and I decided that was her destiny and not mine.

My stepfather had gotten into some trouble, and they decided to pack up and leave. I realized it was more of his decision rather than a mutual agreement between the two of them. I know you probably wonder what kind of mother would leave her daughter out on the streets. Let me clear that up for you. The choice to be on my own was one I made; however, it was the issues that led to that decision that I had no control over.

I somehow felt that he could control her life, but I would no longer give him that power over mine. My stepfather was the kind of man that felt as though it was his way or no way at all, not to mention he was also using drugs. I don't know about you, but living with a drug addict is not the easiest thing in the world to do. There would be times when he would come home and beat my mother for no reason at all. He was a very jealous person that felt as though he could run the streets all night with whomever he chose, and she was to just deal with it. In his mind, she was to stand beside him no matter what. In the Bible, it does call for wives to be submissive to their husbands, but at the same time, husbands are supposed to love and respect their wives as well. So, you see, that day when they decided to leave, I felt as though that was my way of escape from all of the pain of the present circumstances, and I ran away.

In life, everyone has choices, and the choices you make are yours and yours alone. To tell you the truth, this was probably the best and the worst thing that could happen to me, all in one. Even though it did leave me with emotional scars, it played a key role in shaping my future. The one thing about emotional scars is that you have to be extremely careful with them; if not, they can make you bitter. This type of pain can start to become a part of who you are and define how you view life. Hurt, pain, tests, and trials were never intended to stop you from achieving your dreams. God allows us to endure these encounters so that we can learn from them and grow in him.

It would have been so much easier for me to quit. I was out in the world and all alone. Yeah, I had friends, but the love of a friend can never amount to that of a parent. My sister was about six months old, and with a new baby in the picture, it was as though they had a family of their own. That's how it felt to me. Don't get me wrong; I don't mean to sound selfish; I love my sister dearly. I felt so fortunate. We are sixteen years apart, and I loved the thought of having someone to whom I could be an inspiration.

It's just that my stepfather wanted what he wanted when he wanted it, and he usually got just that. I would always question why my mother let him run her life the way she did. As I told you earlier, I never lived with my mother growing up. I could not stand the constant fighting. Waking out of my sleep to her screaming because he was hitting her. The older I got, the more I began to see that she was terrified of him. In my opinion, men that hit women are cowards. They have low self-esteem, and the only way for them to feel some sense of validation is to tear down someone else. The Bible says, "for whatsoever a man soweth, that shall he also reap" (Galatians 6:7). Well, it is one thing to reap seeds that you sowed into your future, but reaping someone else's is a whole different ball game.

When I decided to leave home, it was my chance to try and put some closure to my past and start over. I had no idea where I would go or what I would do for food. At the age of 17, I was essentially homeless. The one thing that helped me through was a deep sense of knowing that I would be just fine. I would not advise anyone to make the choices I made, but I will tell you to follow your heart.

Often you can get confused and not know what you want or what way you should go. The word of God clearly states, "My sheep hear my voice, and I know them, and they follow me" (John 10:27). That is what it means to follow your heart because God speaks to the heart. The heart's answer to any problem is most likely the one thing we don't want to do.

Don't mistake it; the Bible never calls for us to be disobedient, and that is clearly what I was, but that was my path, and we all have one. Would I have been able to encourage someone else with my life experiences if I had not left? Who knows?

You must grab hold of your destiny and find your way through the challenges that have been set before you. It is not good for you or me to walk someone else's path. In doing so, we will always end up in the wrong place.

Once everything was said and done, and what I knew as a family was gone, it began to sink in. Lord, what am I to do? I was a few months away from starting my senior year in high school. All I had were the clothes left behind in the house for me, and my mother had called a friend of mine and advised her to let me know I should go and pick them up. I had nowhere to sleep and no money.

Understand people have all the advice you think you need until you're in the middle of the situation. It's as though I was on a remote island alone, and the one boat left for me had been broken in two by the waves that beat up against the shore. Imagine that boat being your only way to civilization, and you are with no food, water, or open line of communication with the world that lies on the other side of the water.

I went and gathered my things all alone and called up my aunt and cousin that lived nearby to see if I could stay for a while. They took me in, but it was nothing like I thought it would be. It's so easy to deal with family until you need them. So there I was, wondering about loss and thinking about how

I would survive. Who would enroll me in school? What would I eat? Was it okay that I lived there?

I remember sitting in my cousins' driveway one night praying and looking up at the stars. I had never seen a falling star before. As I began to talk to God, I started to express to him how that was something I had longed to experience as a kid. Every time one would fall when I was a child, and someone would mention it, it was gone by the time I looked up. I talked to God that day, looking up with tears in my eyes, hurt in my heart, and no words on my lips. I began to express how that faith I had always been taught to hold on to at that moment was slipping away.

The night was quiet and still, no noise, not even a cricket. It seemed as if even the wind stood still. As I listened, I heard a voice on the inside say, "Look up!" As I looked up, a falling star began to light up across the sky. It was the most beautiful thing I had ever experienced. Then another and another. It was like a firework show. That day my faith went to another level, a level that, at the time, I never knew would be the very thing that would keep me sane as I walked the path before me.

I finally felt I had what I needed to keep moving. It's like I got a second wind, a breath of life that held me up just when I felt like quitting. I wasn't sure at that point how long my cousin would allow me to stay, but it was mid-summer, and school hadn't started, so there was still time.

I continued to live there for a while until one day my time was up. I was back in the position of having to find somewhere else to go. Oh, no! Not again. I had changed residence three times already, and the school year was starting. I kept telling myself I had to finish high school. I just refused to be a statistic. I was far too intelligent to stop shy of receiving my high school diploma. I geared up. I got myself together and made a conscious decision that I would finish no matter what.

I was able to get enrolled for my senior year without a guardian to sign any paperwork. Only God knows, to this day, how that happened and to Him be the glory for it all. I am grateful daily that he has always had his hands on me. I am very tenacious by nature. If you tell me what I can't do, that's all the motivation I need to prove I can. I worked hard! I didn't miss one day of my senior year. Looking back over that time frame, I can remember the struggle. I can remember every emotion.

First, I went from living with one family member to the next. Then I lived with my friend, who had recently graduated high school two years prior and was rooming with her best friend, Tia. They had been generous enough to let me sleep on their couch. Next, Shantel would get up every morning, take me to school, and pick me up every evening. With her as my angel and my persistence to finish school, I went every day.

I like to think of myself as intelligent, but I had fallen a bit behind due to my troubled home life. So, for me to graduate on time, I had to work extra hard. I was determined to do it with or without a parent to push or oversee my studies. This was something I knew I had to accomplish. It would be the first thing in my life that I ever had to be proud of myself.

My math teacher at the time was such an angel. He would encourage me daily, telling me how bright I was. But he knew what I was going through, and it put me on edge. I questioned what would happen if anyone else found out. So, I prayed that he kept my secret. I feared that it might cause problems for me if someone found out and hinder me from receiving my diploma.

Well, guess what? I did it! I finally made it, and I graduated high school! But, boy, was it a rough road, not to mention a long one.

Reflections

1. When you think about abandonment, what is the first emotion you feel?

2. What are areas of your life tied to feelings of abandonment?

3. How do you deal with these areas or issues in your life?

4. Do your abandonment issues affect your relationships or goals?

5. Does it hinder your success? If so, in what ways?

6. Who or where would you be if you released the distraction of abandonment?

Distraction 3:

LOSS

"The state or feeling of grief when deprived of someone or something of value."

"To lose is not a loss at all; it's the open door to new possibilities and the pathway to fulfillment"

— Mel Jackson.

I was finally out of high school and out on my own. I was working and living with roommates paying bills. I had a man in my life, which probably wasn't the best situation for me at the time. Once again, I had lost focus, walking along this road, trying to find my way. Through trial and error, I was desperate to see where I fit. What does God truly have in store for me?

I was partying and living life to the fullest. I was taking pills to cope with my inner guilt and shame. I told myself I took them just because I liked how they made me feel and, not to mention, my friends were taking them. I didn't take hard-core drugs, just prescription meds that I need not name. Looking back, I know I was taking them to run from my pain. Temporarily they made me forget about everything I was dealing with or had dealt with, for that matter. Living life by the seat of my pants, I found myself pregnant. How in the world was I going to care and provide for a baby?

I have always wanted children. I felt that would fill this void I had in my life. One thing I feared I would never experience was someone to love me unconditionally. At the same time, I was terrified because I never wanted my children to experience the disappointments I had encountered in my past. By no stretch of the imagination did I get pregnant on purpose. I just believed that since it happened, nothing could make me happier.

We both were very young and not married, so you can imagine what that was like for me. He had two children at an early age, now 21 and working on number three. I was not proud of being pregnant at this age, but, hey, we all make mistakes.

It's true that the worst mistakes ever made are those from which you took no lesson.

— Mel Jackson

Pregnant, living from place to place, and friend to friend, I was very uncomfortable. I was not willing to let that interfere with becoming the woman God had destined me to be. I made up my mind that I would be the best mother that a child could ever have. I would give my seed so much more than my mother gave me on a compassionate level. You see, you can give a child all the material things that money can buy, but if there is no compassion or bond between a child and a parent, it is all in vain.

Well, as always, I was in for a real life changing experience. I started to think this was becoming the story of my life; for every ounce of joy, there would be ten pounds of pain. I walked into my doctor's appointment, barely into my second trimester, to have a sonogram. If only I had known that when I rolled out of bed that morning, my life would be changed forever, maybe, I would have stayed asleep. You never know what life has to offer until something unexpectedly slaps you in the face.

When I laid down on that table, I was all excited about getting to explore what is living inside of me. It's a lot like a personal invitation to a life that that's waiting to bloom. Well, unfortunately for me, that happy moment turned into one of the worst moments of my life. While the nurse was examining me, I could tell something was wrong. It was one of those situations where you're sitting waiting for some results, and the atmosphere around just lets you know something's not quite right. If you've been there, then you know what I mean. It feels like everything around you goes still, and you're watching life in slow motion. You could probably hear my heart beating from four blocks away. I was a nervous wreck. My body was still, and my hands were as cold as ice from fear.

Then, she said to me, "Ms. Jackson, we have a problem. Something is going on with the way the baby is developing, and we need to have you checked by a specialist."

I was sitting there thinking, Lord, I am here all alone, and this lady is telling me something is wrong with my child. You will have to help me with this one. I was seriously trying to stay calm as she was explaining the process to me. There was fluid around the sack that holds the baby, and it was a little more than usual. She continued to explain that while taking the baby's measurements, something just wasn't adding up. She told me there was no need to be alarmed just yet because it could be non-life-threatening to my child or me. They just had to send me to a specialist to be sure.

She asked me to sit up and make myself comfortable, and she would be right back with the details and directions to the office of the specialist I was to see. At the time, I just needed someone to talk to—somebody, anybody, please. You are probably asking yourself, where was that faith that kicked in when your mother left three years ago because the same God that delivered me could walk me through this.

I did not want to walk. I needed to be carried. This burden was heavy. I was only 20 years old. I was still trying to figure out life and trying to sort out how I would even be a parent in my mind. Now, this!

I pleaded with God to please give me a break. How much can one take? How many more crosses would I have to bear and bear alone? I was screaming inside for God to please HELP me. It was then that I knew the true meaning of the poem, "Footprints in the Sand," when there was only one set, and God said, "It was then that I carried you."

You see, even though God is all we need, sometimes it does help to have a physical person to lean on as well. We all need a little support from time-to-time. I don't know about you, but there are times in your life when enduring certain things, you need a shoulder to cry on and a hand to hold. I don't mean to offend anyone, but let's be honest, people always say pray about it, but sometimes you get to a stage where you don't want to pray. It's as if you say, can somebody pray for me this time because I don't have the strength to do it myself. So, I called my cousin Marion. She was older and more like an aunt whom I admired. She was a prayer warrior that knew all about trusting God. It was the calmness in her voice and her warm words of encouragement that gave me the extra strength I needed to go to the next doctor's appointment.

I walked into that appointment not knowing what to expect, but all I could think was, God, not my will, but allow your will to be done in my life. Well, that day, I was given a choice. I was told that my daughter had a fifty-fifty chance for survival, and at that point, I could terminate my pregnancy. I sat in that room quietly, not knowing if I should scream, cry or give up altogether. I was so scared and confused. That's when the questions started, "Lord, why me?"

I was taught we should never question God. Yet, as I sat in this empty place, I needed an answer, and I needed it right then. I could not wait for it. I was not willing to let it be put on hold. I was confused, and I was scared. Pleading, "God help me to understand this mess," I wasn't sure what I should do. I had no clue how this story would end. Thoughts were racing through my head. If I decided to continue the pregnancy, and the baby didn't make it, would I be able to live with that? If I terminated the pregnancy, would I be able to live the rest of my life not knowing? I decided to go through with the pregnancy, putting all my trust in God to have the last say because I knew I would never be at peace with wondering, and it was never really my decision to make. I would leave this one totally up to him, and he would do what was best.

You see, he will never put more on you than you can bear. Yeah, I know this was a heavy burden, but he said, "Cast all your cares on me" (1 Peter 5:7), "for my yoke is easy, and my burden is light" (Matthew 11:30), so that's what I did. It was hard to do, especially when dealing with the odds of my child's life at stake.

From that day forward, I was scheduled for appointments once every two weeks to measure the baby's growth. Every time I went in, I walked out with the same devastating results, but I had no choice but to keep believing.

As the saying goes, "when life hands your lemons, you make lemonade." In other words, you must keep your faith because it outweighs the fear. Doing this allows you to have peace even when the outcome is not what you wanted. Standing on your faith is like a dress rehearsal for the opening night of a musical on Broadway. For some, it will be the most significant production of their life. Not knowing what to expect or how many people will be waiting in the audience when the curtain rolls back. Even amid the questions and uncertainties, you gather yourself and proceed forward, trusting that it will all work in your favor.

It was Thanksgiving Day 1999. After all of the turkey, I got home from visiting with my family, and I started feeling weird. I was warned that I could go into preterm labor from previous trips to the doctor due to the excessive amino acids. My cousin and I were roommates at the time, but she was downstairs, passed out on the couch, so I took the keys and drove myself to the hospital. I was there for hours, and no one even knew where I was. I attempted to call several people, and no one answered, so I just waited.

Finally, I called up my friend I nicknamed Truth because no matter what, she always kept it real. Over the years, she had become like my big sister. No matter where I was or what I was going through, she was always there for me. If there was one thing I could be sure of, it was that she would come anytime I called. I told her that I had been admitted into the hospital, and I was there all alone, and I was scared.

Within the hour, she was right there and sat with me until the end. Even though the doctor had explained that this could happen, I was barely seven months into my pregnancy, and if you've ever had a child, you know that a woman should not be in labor just yet. So, I lay there in the hospital bed patiently waiting to see what was going on, and the nurses kept coming in to check on me. I went in on Thursday, and I was still there on Saturday. I awoke from my sleep at about 6:30 am Saturday morning November 27, 1999. My bed was a little wet, so I called for the nurse. I informed her that I could not make it to the restroom (it couldn't have been more than a foot away) without wetting my underwear. By 6:30 pm (12 hours later), they performed a test to see if my water had broken, and indeed it had.

To this day, I still have no clue why it took 12 hours to figure that out, but that was the least of my worries. The specialist I was seeing was about 30 miles away at Harris Methodist Hospital in Fort Worth, TX, and he had left specific instructions in my file for when I went into labor. I was to be transported to him immediately. This hospital was equipped to handle children with special needs. They said that delivering there would give the baby a better chance for survival.

As I was getting ready to be transported by ambulance, I was once again all alone. I rode to the hospital with Jesus holding my hand and a stranger talking to me. One of the paramedics was a woman who had given birth a few times herself, and she was nice enough to ride in the back with me. To this day, in my book, she must have been an angel. She had such a loving personality.

After a few wrong turns, we were 20 minutes out of the way, but we finally made it to our destination. Yes, we got lost from one hospital to the next. On top of everything that I was going through in the back, the ambulance driver had no clue where he was going, which only added to the frustration. We all have taken a wrong turn in life, but we can always end up at our destination with prayer and a self-check.

Once I was all settled in, they started the preparations for delivery, but then noticed that the baby had an irregular heartbeat. Her heart was beating so fast, they had to induce my labor and take her immediately. Understand that before arriving at the specialty hospital, for three days, the other hospital had been giving me a medication that stops a pregnant woman from having Braxton Hicks (false labor) contractions. Giving me any medication was something that my doctor had advised should not be done. He made it very clear beforehand that there would be nothing done to save my daughter, possibly putting my health or life at risk. I tried telling the nurses that on several occasions, but they would not listen to me.

My regular doctor was out on vacation, and the doctor on call for him had advised that they do whatever they felt would be best. If you question where the baby's father is during all this havoc, I am still unsure. Some say they saw him at the club that night. All I know is that he left the hospital after being there maybe a total of 30 minutes and said that he would be back. Yes, I was still in labor at that point. I was lying there in bed, in an enormous amount of pain, and if you've ever been there, I know you feel me.

I started to bleed out from my womb, so it was too late for an Epidural. The only thing I had to aid me was Demerol, and trust me, that is not enough when you are experiencing that kind of pain. "Oh my God"! On top of all this, they tell me that the baby had not turned, and they did not have time to turn her, so I would have to give birth to a breech baby. You all know that the head and shoulders are the most complex part of giving birth to mothers. From that point, it's usually straightforward. Well, that's what they say, but I never had a chance to experience that because my baby came out just the opposite. They say that they did not want me to have a cesarean because they refused to do anything that might harm me to save the baby, given the odds in the beginning.

After a rough time in delivery, I gave birth to a baby girl. She was two pounds nine ounces. I named her Zatavia, which was a name Truth had picked out for me. I just loved it because it reminded me of a flower, and that is what she was to me, my flower. If you have ever walked across a field in the springtime, the flowers make it look so peaceful. I am a country girl, and I loved all the freshly bloomed flowers.

The hard part was over. All the pain had stopped, and now what? I waited until the whole room was silent, my heart skipped a beat, and my feet grew numb. I had never given birth before, but I was sure that the sweetest sound in the world is that of your baby's first cry for any new mother. For me, that never happened, and that is when the pain began.

At that point, I realized that giving birth was nothing compared to what I was now facing. Yeah, I know that this was always possible, but it never really set in until I got to that point. My eyes watered. My heart ached as I waited.

Then, I heard those words, "I am sorry, Ms. Jackson. She didn't make it."

Do you mean to tell me after all this hell, this is what I get? I was confused, depressed, dismantled, but there are no words to describe how going through that made me feel. I would watch new mothers as they strolled through the hospital, and I saw the joy in their eyes, which made me sick to my stomach.

Through my pain, I became very materialistic. I used shopping to compensate for my inner struggles. I poured everything that I had into what I looked like on the outside, trying to camouflage what I was going through on the inside and never wanting anyone to see the real me. I honestly didn't even want to tap into my pain. It hurt too deeply to look into the mirror and see myself for who I was—used, abused, angry, hostile, and fragile. If anyone tried to correct me, I would often become defensive and defended every action made, justifying to myself that I had every reason to feel and act as I please.

Waking up every day, I tried to convince me that life would get better if I kept moving. I learned how to store my pain versus shelving it. The difference is when you delay pain, you always go back to it and deal with it. You just put it away for the time being until you feel comfortable enough to deal with it. Well, when you store it, you tuck it away in deep places, trying to hide it so deep that it never resurfaces. To my surprise, I learned that it always resurfaces. It has a way of presenting itself just when we least expect it. In my life, it began to come out as anger, pride, low self-esteem, confusion, and so many other things that if I listed them, it would take days, if not weeks. Let's say, the more I ran from my issues, the emotional hole I dug for myself just got more profound, and I was going to have to claw my way out.

I just wanted to be loved. I needed to be loved. I needed someone who would stand with me at all cost. I needed someone who wouldn't talk behind my back or throw me away when I could no longer benefit them. I guess what I really needed was me. I needed to fall in love with myself inside and out on a level so deep that it no longer mattered who came or stayed. I needed to build a bond with myself that was so tight, you couldn't pry it apart. I needed God to show me what love was, and I needed to admit to myself that I had no clue at all.

Reflections

1. What or who have you lost that you feel affected you intensely?

2. How do you deal with loss, or how have you dealt with it in the past?

3. Is anyone or anything you lost still inflicting hurt upon you at this moment?

4. How does exposing these situations make you feel?

5. What advice would you give someone to comfort them in their time of loss?

6. List three people in your life that have/will support you during your time of loss.

Distraction 4:

PAIN

"Physical suffering or discomfort caused by illness or injury."

"Pain is inevitable. Suffering is optional."
— Buddhist proverb

Sifting and navigating through pain can be a process. It would be so much easier to move through life and never deal with hurt, be it physical or emotional. Pain is something that will keep you up at night. It will make you ball up in a fetal position and clutch your pearls. I've seen It break the strongest men to their knees. It will humble you and make you rethink every decision and encounter you've ever had.

To me, one of the worst things about pain is that you have to hurt to heal. Everyone wants to be on the other side of things that they find utterly unbearable, yet we fail to acknowledge and welcome the fact that we have to go through the process to reach the other side. I have been at what seemed to be the top of the world and bottom at the same time. One thing about pain is that it doesn't care where you're from or where you live.

There is nothing worse than being crippled and tormented by the pain of your past. Every time you get up and catch your breath, life can hand you things that knock you down again. After you've been knocked down time after time, you can become numb to the process. At that point, I believe that it becomes a familiar place. When things are going great, you tend to walk around on eggshells, waiting for something to go wrong. It's not because it's what you are hoping for. It's merely because you become familiar with devastation. That's the worst thing one can do.

Having so many experiences that were devastating I became one with a place that births self-fulfilling prophecies that speak against my destiny. I was walking around on edge, afraid that every great thing in my life will be followed by tragedy. This mindset became a constant place for me. Imagine the emotional turmoil of being up and down at the same time, yet still having to operate from a space where you shelve the hurt in front of people with the hopes that no one sees it. My wound was so deep that I buried it beneath the scars and bruises of my ego. I told myself that I could never be vulnerable or open enough to allow people to see me because it opened the door to more pain and more heartache.

There I was, running in a house of mirrors again, trying to recover from the tragedies of my past and trying not to relive the desolate place that housed my most horrifying experiences. Why did it seem that everything in my life that was seemingly good was a setup for more abandonment? The things that I tried to convince myself would build character and strengthen me kept hurting me. I was running and standing still all at the same time. I had escaped one place of grief, and another met me at the door. I was looking for something that I could never seem to find.

Let me be the first to say I thought what I needed to validate myself could be found in people. I was going from one horrible relationship to the next. Do know, these relationships were not always intimate relationships with a man. Sometimes they were friendships that I held on to, and they kept crippling me, ripping me apart at the seam and leaving me feeling used up and confused.

I begged God at times to harden my heart so I could no longer care for people or give them access to my love or loyalty because I felt like I was being gutted open like a fish every time they talked about me, lied to me, or misunderstood my intentions. Finally, I realized one day I had stumbled upon the one thing I never wanted to be, and that was a reflection of what I saw my mother go through. The thought of it hurt to the core.

The more I fought to avoid that outcome, the closer it drew near to me. Finally, I found myself at a dead-end street, and I didn't have enough gas to turn around. Here I was again in an entanglement that served me like a bartender ignoring the client's limits that had way too many drinks. I kept feeding on the thing that was eating away at me, victimized by my inability to love myself from a pure place, and placing the blame on the people that I had allowed to hurt me yet again. You see, my most significant setback was loving the wrong people from the wrong place. I was trying to love from the place where I needed to be loved. The only example I had of the type of love I longed for was the one I had created from a place that paralyzed me.

I was a people pleaser always wanting to be liked by everyone and never be misunderstood. I made a lot of mistakes in this place. Again and again I was beating myself up while I sat and questioned myself. I Often screamed to the top of my lungs, praying I didn't lose any more of myself or my mind sifting through the process. Tragedy struck again and again, and I tried to find a way out. There had to be a way out, and I had to keep pushing. I had to keep praying. I had to keep talking.

Can someone please help me? Is anyone listening to me? Does anyone see or feel what I am going through? Or does anyone even care? God save me from me. I had spent more time praying over my life than I ever had before, and I was truly living and enjoying life at this point. Oh, I know this is not a bad thing at all. I just wanted absolute joy and total peace. I no longer wanted to live in turmoil. The pain was just too unbearable.

If you have ever experienced this, you know it can be hard finding someone willing to listen or admit that they understand. So let me be the first to say, you are not alone. I see you. I hear you, and I am a living witness that I understand. I understand how your soul can cry out from a hard place for your mind to comprehend. It doesn't make you crazy or mentally unstable—it makes you human. You're supposed to feel emotions, and know that is okay. What you can't do is become institutionalized by pain and suffering. You can't become what you go through. You must allow the experiences to build you. Allow them to shift you. If we do more shifting in emotions rather than sifting through emotions, we can become healthy.

I remember reading *Battlefield of the Mind* by Joyce Meyer not even really realizing or understanding that I was in a battle myself. I picked it up at the bookstore obviously because my spirit knew something that my mind and my heart hadn't begun to comprehend. I was in the biggest battle of my life. If I could make it through the painful moments, I could start to encourage myself from a different place. I could begin to recognize when I was in danger emotionally or physically. I could make some better decisions along the way, proceeding with caution in every situation rather than walking in fear, creating an atmosphere where I began to protect myself, and being proactive often rather than reactive.

You see, the mind is powerful. It's proven that we become what we think. Then who we become is what we seek in others and experiences. So, if you become a victim, you desire to be victimized. If you become angry, you begin seeking experiences that will feed that anger.

Reflections

1. What areas of your life have caused you pain?
2. When you think back, what emotions did you experience while dealing with painful situations?
3. How has pain affected your growth?
4. What are you saying to yourself daily?
5. How does what you say to yourself help you in unfortunate situations?

Distraction 5:

PERCEPTION

"A way of regarding, understanding, or interpreting something."

"Change the way you look at things, and the things you look at change."
— Wayne W. Dyer

Perception is everything. It shapes and molds who you become. It lies dormant at the surface of every decision you make. How you see yourself is the most critical view of life you'll ever have the pleasure of knowing. It can haunt you in the middle of the night. It's the thing that will cause you to lay awake, questioning who and what you are meant to be. Yet, more than anything, it will affect every decision you make.

My perception of life has always been full of energy and fear, all at the same time. Even when I thought I was sure of the promises spoken over my life. Perception has always crept in, in the back of my mind. It laid dormant like a lion ready to roar or a bee sting preparing to swell. Being shaped and molded by every encounter, good or bad.

It was Easter weekend 2012. A few months prior, I had hooked back up with one of my girlfriends from my past. We'll call her Jazz to protect her real identity. You must understand that Jazz is very strong-willed, determined, and loves to travel. She had been mentioning to me for weeks that she wanted to take a weekend getaway to clear her head because she worked so much. So, we decide to take a trip just to have some good girly fun.

I will admit, I was not interested in going, although I probably really needed it. Jazz had been researching airline tickets for weeks and was so excited. She finally found tickets, and when it came time to purchase, I honestly didn't want to go. We sat debating for hours on the phone with me trying to find an alternative, while Jazz contested every suggestion I made. Finally, I gave in. I said those dreadful words, "I'll let you decide, and I'll roll with it."

Jazz purchased her ticket, so I was stuck. There was no way I could let her go alone, or her money would go to waste, so I clicked the button, entered in my credit card information, and we were on our way.

As the days approached leading up to our trip, I was still uneasy about it. Then, I got a call from a friend of mine who traveled daily for his profession. In general conversation, he asked what I was doing for Easter weekend. I went on ranting and raving about how Jazz had talked me into taking a trip, which I had no interest in going on. He then expressed that he would be in the area for work that very same weekend, and we could hook up according to his schedule. That made me start feeling a bit better about the trip. After all, he was like a brother to me, so I just knew with him around, I would have a fantastic time.

On the second day of the trip, he decided to take us to dinner. After dinner, to my surprise, he mentioned that there was someone he wanted me to meet. I was totally against the idea. I had been through so many failed dating experiences that the last thing I needed was to be hooked up. He had a friend that he had been talking to about me for some time, and finally, he had us in the same city.

I finally gave in to the idea, thinking it couldn't be all that bad if I remained optimistic. Besides, what could it hurt? I wasn't looking for anything serious. I just wanted to have fun. Then, I met Ricky! It excited me to my very core. He had exceptional brown skin and was extremely tall and handsome. Then, to top it all off, he had the most amazing smile that made my heart skip a beat or two. He was dressed simply in blue sweatpants and a black t-shirt. The funny thing is that I saw him after dinner as we were entering the hotel lobby. I ignored every gesture from him in hopes of getting my attention. I saw him stop and stare out of the corner of my eye, but I had no time to be meeting anyone in my mind. I was good.

All my past experiences with men and every failed encounter had called for a much-needed break. So, when my friend called him downstairs to meet me, unbeknownst to me, it was the same guy I had previously ignored getting on the elevator. We made light of the situation, laughing it off before engaging in some more meaningful conversation. I must admit, I just knew I had met the man of my dreams. Every day I would wake up feeling a sense of love that I had never known before, and with every word, he took me higher and higher.

Finally, God had answered my prayer after all the heartbreak that I had encountered. He had finally sent me someone that I could build with and who treated me like a queen. Daily this man sang to me, and we would engage in lengthy conversations. He was concerned with every area of my life every day. I called him Ike, and he called me Anna Mae. Before you go there, nothing about our relationship was abusive. You may be saying to yourself, why would I even entertain such foolish pet names given the history behind them. It was just our thing, a little joke between us. He was so gentle, so caring, and so loving.

The more I got to know him, the more I loved him. We would talk all day and night and skyped every chance we got. We couldn't get enough of each other. I wore a smile that I had never experienced in my life. The sound of his voice warmed my heart, and the gentleness of his touch soothed my pain. Things were great for months. He shared things with me what was relevant about his past relationships and life, which was all that mattered because we were building something.

For the first time in a long time, I finally trusted some-one. I had finally let someone in, and it felt good. Then, one day I got a text from him following an argument from the day before, and when I began to read it, my heart melted. I had been out shopping all day, and I was leaving the mall. I re-member standing in the parking lot with my mouth open as I paid close attention to every word. He had finally done it! He had finally said the one thing that I longed to hear. He said, "I Love You!"

It brought tears to my eyes. I couldn't believe it. I had escaped so much pain, and I was finally free from what seemed to be endless heartbreaks. If I am to be brutally honest, it scared the hell out of me. Don't get me wrong, I loved him as well, but I would have never expressed it for the sake of protecting myself. Then it started, all the doubt of the possi-ble things that could go wrong. What if it doesn't last? What if he hurts me? What if he's not ready?

I tried to live in the moment while I dealt with a whale of emotions. No one wants to keep coming up empty-handed.

No one wants to keep reliving the emotional fiasco that spirals you down like a tornado when things start to take a turn for the worst. I was old enough to know that sometimes love is not enough. So, I had to question if the love he had for me was enough to stand the test of time. When we met, I remember him telling me that I was the woman of his dreams, and he knew that he wanted it forever.

Once I pulled myself out of Debbie Downer mode, I replied with those words that I never thought I'd ever use again as long as I lived, "I Love you too!"

He was genuinely relieved as it took me a minute to reply. The only response he could muster up was, "You scared me. I thought I had scared you away." Nope, not at all! I have always been a fighter. Everything in my past was evident, so he wasn't going to scare me off that easily. My heart and head had a severe battle with each other, and obviously, my heart won! It managed to convince my head that no matter how much pain it had suffered, it was willing to take a risk. After all, life is all about risk. I will be the first to admit this was the best relationship I had ever encountered at that point. It wasn't because of him or anything he did but because I learned so much about myself.

> *"You have to leave the city of your comfort and go into the wilderness of your intuition. You can't get there by bus, only by hard work and risk and by not quite knowing what you're doing. What you'll discover will be wonderful. What you'll discover will be yourself."* — **Alan Alda**

The above quote is near and dear to me. The truth is love hurts, and relationships take work. We tend to fall into a pattern of what we want others to be rather than accepting people for who they are. We would love to look at them as if looking in a mirror and see a reflection of ourselves. It's in doing so that it puts to bed all of the fear and uncertainties of the unknown.

So often we're afraid to let those we love be who they indeed are for fear that they will realize we somehow don't fit into the picture that they have created for themselves. This place where my emotions were residing was a place of un-surety and uncertainty. It was a place that was empty and exhausted, one that had nothing else to give to anything that wasn't con-nected to my future.

I was so tired of meaningless experiences. I refused to let anyone else take advantage of, or take for granted, the great woman I was becoming. I had no time for emotional setbacks. I was no longer willing to settle or entertain the idea of long nights, heartaches, and tears. That is the one thing that is always a possibility when we take a chance on love—any love, for that matter. Yet, I am so grateful I did.

Through the distance and the tough times, I found the missing pieces of the woman I had been looking for the last twelve years of my life. As I said before, I was evolving into this great woman, but I had no idea that some of what helped her on her path to exceptional lay dormant, right in the love upon which I had stumbled.

I began to feel the need for "freedom." Finally, I was in a place in my mind to see the world the way I was meant to see it and understand the things going on around me affecting my day-to-day activities and relationships. I needed a deeper understanding of my life, circumstances, and every encounter that I had experienced, good or bad, so that I could link it to who I was called to be.

Sometimes my perception crippled me. It terrified me because the person that everyone saw on the outside fought battles daily to fit into the same perception that others saw in me. Hiding behind my smile because if people perceived me as happy, then it would change my own perception. I hid behind my relationships because if people perceived me as connected, it would change my perception. I was hiding behind my hurt and my loss because if people could understand what I'd walked through, then it would change my perception of the very things that held me back and that held me bound.

So often, people would criticize every decision I made and every action that I took because to them, those things defined me, but they hurt me deeply. The more hurt I experienced, the more distorted my perception of myself became. With every experience I encountered, each incident became cloudier. So, to the point, at times, I couldn't remember or recall some of the things I had gone through. While writing this book, it triggered so many memories. Certain ones were so horrible that every minute of each replay took something out of me.

I was the star in my motion picture, one that forced me to sit in the theater's front row as it played on the big screen. It was like watching a horror film, but I wasn't fortunate enough to have the luxury of covering my eyes in hopes of not seeing what was coming next. I realized that I had locked my experiences in a closet and hid the key from myself, truly believing that I would no longer be affected by the pain they caused if I never reopened the door. The bad thing is that to be effective, you must acknowledge what has affected you. You must ask yourself, "Do I want to be well known and well-liked while dying on the inside, or do I want to be free?"

Reflections

1. What is your perception of yourself or your current situation?

2. How many times have you allowed your perception to create a false image of who you are?

3. How does your perception affect your day-to-day life?

4. Has your perception hindered you in your career or relationships?

5. Looking over your life, list 5 things that you perceived to be more than what it was?

Distraction 6:

LOVE

"The most important relationship you have is with yourself."
— Alice McCall

"Show Yourself Love Through Forgiveness"

From a place of healthy perceptions, we learn to love without limits, giving us the ability to be free. It allows us to go against the grain, to no longer succumb to or sit in the shadows of the places where fear resides. It gives life and hopes all at once. The most valuable lesson I learned about love was through loss. In three years, I lost more than I had ever imagined. I remember sitting thinking to myself, how can God still use me? Why would these things happen to me? I needed God to show me what love was, and I had to come to terms with the fact that I had no clue at all. Real love is the ability to love from the inside out and not the outside inward.

I had met the love of my life, so I thought. Finally, after all of the failed attempts, he was supportive, understanding, career-driven, and I knew he would always have my back. The connection between us was electrifying. We had so many things in common and bonded on a level no one would ever understand. There were days I was in awe of his treatment of me. As you read previously, I had been in many relationships, and none of them encouraged me, none of them supported or uplifted me, and despite all that, I learned from them all.

Every time one of them took a piece of me, I learned something more about myself. I learned that I was trying to love through pain versus grow through it. By now, you would have thought I no longer had such a desire or need to be loved or accepted by anyone. After all of the setbacks and disappointments, I finally figured out how to navigate through and put myself in a place of peace that would shield and protect my emotions. I asked myself, what am I saving my feelings from? Was it from the people that had hurt me? Or was it from me? I firmly believe that, in some way, I was protecting myself from me and my ability to trust in people to the point where it hurts. I saw the good in everyone from my innocent child-like spirit, not realizing I was only looking at them from the surface level.

You're probably thinking to yourself, "She started this chapter talking about a man, one who was so good and a relationship that seemed so rewarding. How could any of that have a negative side?"

Yes, the relationship was great and rewarding while in each other's presence. It built me up way more than it tore me down. Compared to all of the smokescreen relationships of my past, it was the most authentic. It gave me genuine emotion and support that I longed to have. Being in it allowed me to be vulnerable on a level that would prepare me for what was to come. However, the foundation it was built upon was unstable. The timing was off. If I could have stepped back into time and started over, it would have been a perfect love. It just happened in an imperfect moment.

When it ended after five years, I was right back at the bottom of Abandonment Hill, not because he had left me, but because I abandoned me. I was both free and in bondage all at the same time. I knew what I wanted and what I desired to set me free. Not knowing this was just the beginning of some of the best lessons as the worst moments in life, which held me bound.

I began going to therapy (for the third time in my life). I remember my big sister, Truth, saying to me, "Girl, you don't need no therapy." I had to question it for a second because this would be my third experience. The difference is I used the first two attempts at counseling as a bandage and an outlet for the pain. This time I looked at it as brain surgery and a heart transplant, all at the same time. So, I went anyway because I understood something about my mental state that she would never understand. I understood that I was bruised. I understood that I had lost the ability to see clearly. I understood that my abandonment issues were real, and I needed to heal. I needed to sort through the hurt. I needed God to give me peace. I also understood that, in order for that to happen, I needed to change the perception of myself. I needed to see myself as a victor and not a victim.

I could quote the scriptures, and I truly believed them in my heart, yet I was still unstable my emotions. I was being tormented by every decision leading up to this point. Looking in the mirror, I was mentally drained and exhausted. If you could diagnose my condition, the prognosis would have said that my heart filled with pride and peace.

I'll explain. Pride was holding me captive because I felt that, once again, the world could use my inability to flourish in certain areas of my life against me. Peace was knowing that even with tears in my eyes and distorted perception, God would still use me, even though I questioned his ability to. Maybe you've never known God to the point where you believed him and asked questions at the same time. Or perhaps, you are too prideful to admit it for fear of how people will look at you. You see, for me, I desire freedom more than I want people at this point in life. Note I said I "desire" because I didn't say that it always showed in my actions.

The "perfect" relationship had ended, and I was in therapy . . . again. I was learning, growing, and beginning to sort through the hurt. Yet, to my surprise, what I thought was terrible, would only get worse. On June 8, 2019, I lost my big sister, Truth. I lost her to perception—the perception of what someone else believed to be reality. It was a dangerous place where action outweighed the ability to be rational, yet, this perception was one I could not fix. We had been to the casino, which was something we enjoyed doing together. We had the time of our lives. To my surprise, while we were enjoying quality time, she was going through marital problems. One thing about her is that even during the trouble and chaos she experienced, she went to grave lengths to protect me. She never truly wanted me to know what she was going through. We left the casino around 12:45 am and made it back to her car at around 1:30 am. We both had about a 20-30 min drive home. We made plans to go home and nap, and she was going to come over the next day to help me get caught up on some overdue work. So, we decided to meet later that day, around 11 am, at my house. I remember watching her from my rearview mirror until she was out of sight not knowing that it would be the last time I would see her alive.

After picking up my goddaughter, Simone, from a friend's house, we proceeded to drive home. I remember going and having this horrible pain in my chest halfway home. I told her it might have been from the smoke in the casino. I thought maybe after I got home and showered, I would feel better, so, I went home and showered. While in the shower, I missed a few calls from Truth's daughter, Princess. I thought it was strange seeing all the missed calls but only for a second. Princess had just had a baby about a year ago. I was there when she had him and cut the umbilical cord, all while Truth cringed and screamed from behind the curtain in the hospital room. Hey, but that's a story for another day and time. Just know she was tough until her baby girl went into labor, and there was nothing she could do. If you read the earlier chapter, she was also in the room when I gave birth to my daughter and reacted the same way.

I assumed my niece might have been calling at that hour because the baby was not feeling well or something. I kept him a lot when he was a newborn, and her mom worked an early shift. In my mind, she may have been calling for direction or advice with the baby and didn't want to disturb her mom's sleep. Looking back, I wish it would have been that simple. I tried returning my niece's call several times, and her phone went to voicemail, so, I let it go. I never once thought to call her mom being she lived in the house with her. The next call I received was from the father of my niece's children stating that my niece had called him, and he was pretty sure she said that her stepdad had just murdered her mom.

I went numb.

I couldn't believe it to be true. I rationalized in my mind that there was no way because we were just together. I had just left her. But it was true, and my life was forever changed, once again. I won't get into any further details of that situation, but, what I will say is it crushed me and broke my heart.

My mind was racing, and my body was numb. I couldn't speak, I couldn't eat, we had so many plans. But, Lord, how Lord, why? That is what I screamed out in my head over and over, but my mouth would not make a sound. Have you ever been hurt to the point where you know you're alive, and you know you're living in reality, but it's like the world stops and you're stuck? I felt paralyzed. I could hear people talking. I could feel the tears running down my face, but I couldn't utter a word.

Imagine someone taking the life of someone you love and threatening the lives of others. Then, imagine that person having the audacity to call you afterward. I still remember the conversation. I remember the exact time of the call. For a year, I heard it constantly in my head. "Hello, Truth?"

Everything went quiet and then. "Hello, Melonie?"

I was in pure disbelief, as my heart felt like it was slowly being ripped from my chest. Then came the words, "I want you to know, Truth loves you, and she appreciates everything you've done for her and us, but what just happened here we can't come back from. So, we just need you to pray for us."

It pierced my soul. I remember screaming, "Wait! Wait! What do you mean?" Then the call disconnected. It was over. I was left with a million questions.

No, God! She can't be gone! This can't be happening! I'm nervous, trembling, and trying to get dressed all while calling 911. I raced to my car so that I could make my way to their house. I was shaking as I tried to drive. My head was filled with a million thoughts, waiting for that call to confirm it was a mistake. It never came. To this day, I've waited for someone or something to ensure it's not true.

I tried rationalizing in my head what would make him take her life and his own. I've been forced to focus on the good times we shared and accept the answer will never come. Now living in a reality of what was and what used to be. Left only to celebrate the memories of her life and the love she showed to so many. There is not one day that goes by that I don't think of her.

Daily I tried to accept the space I was forced to live in as reality. I was trying to learn to navigate devastation once again, praying one day and doubting the next. I truly felt like I had become "Doubting Thomas" from the bible days (John 20:24-29). How can a God so good and so merciful allow such tragedy? I found myself praying daily and no longer praying for understanding but for peace. I needed peace to get through this. I needed to get in the presence of the only one that could take the pain away.

Reflections

1. In what area of your life have you experienced trauma?

2. What emotions did you feel while in your state of trauma?

3. How many times in your life have you given someone (time, attention, affection, etc.) that they had not earned or deserved from you?

4. How do you gauge who deserves the inner parts of you?

5. After reading the previous chapter, did it change how you would typically gauge who was deserving of this part of you?

6. Have you ever given love credit for something that was just an imitation of what your heart truly desires?

7. How have you learned to determine the difference between authentic love versus an imitation of your heart's desires?

Distraction 7:

FORGIVENESS

Forgiveness by definition:
Stop feeling angry or resentful toward someone
for an offense, flaw, or mistake.

"True forgiveness is when you can say, 'Thank you for that experience.'"
— Oprah Winfrey

I was still in therapy, thriving. I was trying to sort through the pain, navigating my way through the heavy moments and working to find understanding, learning to forgive once again a person responsible for taking a piece of what seemed to be my soul when he took my sister.

As a child, I remember being told to forgive and forget. So, I grew up thinking that's what forgiveness was all about. In a sense, I believed that to forgive someone, all I had to do was say, "I forgive you," and then start my quest to forget what they did to me or how their actions affected my life. Today, I can say, after all I've encountered and the growth I've experienced, that statement can set one up for failure. If you were taught to live by that same principle, I'm sure you're asking me how so?

Well, it just isn't that easy, especially when life continues to hand you lemons, and everyone expects you to make lemonade. Being one who has always smiled through my pain, people tend to forget that I am human and that I still hurt. My spirituality keeps me humble and guides my ability to love. However, that doesn't mean that the actions of others do not anger me. That does not make it any easier not to question God's plan or a series of events or a single encounter.

Just nine months after Truth's death, on March 3, 2020, I lost my grandmother. Talk about a setup for failure. It was Tuesday morning. My grandmother had been sick for about six years, at this point, fighting one health battle after the next. I can say the more she resisted, the happier it seemed she became. She was the apple of my eye, and I learned so much watching her endure one health obstacle after another.

The beginning of this battle started on the day she had her first major stroke in 2014. I remember racing home to check on her. When I made it to the hospital and walked into the room there, she lay helpless but still full of life. The stroke had affected her right side, and she couldn't even brush her teeth on her own. Plagued by immobility and staring in the face of defeat, she smiled at me. They sent a physical therapist every day for three days, and none of them were sure if she would ever walk again, so I just kept praying over her and speaking life over her all while verbally talking to her.

As they worked with her, I encouraged her. I would give her a toothbrush every morning and tell her to brush her teeth. I could see and feel the frustration with every request, and because she always nurtured and cared for me, I desired to do it for her. I questioned why I chose to torment her with the very thing that held her bound. Even though it was in her best interest, and that was not at all the intention. In my heart, I knew she was a fighter. I knew that my presence and encouragement, with God's grace and favor, would help her to pull through it. So, I kept talking to her. They would get her out of bed. I would sit in a chair in front of her. I would coach her to keep walking towards the sound of my voice. In three days, she was walking. In three days, God had moved on my behalf. He had shown me that he would always be with us (Matt 28:20). All we needed to do was stay the course.

I remember my grandmother telling me that God had assured her that he would let her stay a bit longer. This was six years before she passed. I had no idea how much longer that "little while" would be. I never thought that time would expire on March 3, 2020. I remember all of the times she had been sick before. I would pray and plead that if I lost my grandmother, I would lose my mind. I couldn't imagine life without her, not for one moment. When I lost my grandmother, she was so precious to me that I became resentful. There were days that I was upset with her for leaving me. If you're not careful, you can grow cold and numb in those moments.

"To forgive means you have released yourself from past places and the people that hurt you. It is an indication that you are ready to move on and embrace the present moment."
— The Art of Forgiveness by Mindview Psychology

The truth is, it was freeing to know that my grandmother was no longer suffering, but losing her came with a bit of resentment. It came with many questions that didn't follow with the answers I felt I needed to find comfort. She was my best friend and someone that never passed judgment on me. Her love for me was the purest form of love I had ever known. She knew things about me that she would never speak openly. No matter what I did, she still believed in me. No matter how low I was, she still encouraged me. In her eyes, I was the apple of her eye. She taught me to smile no matter what, no matter how much it hurt or what people said about me. So, when she left this world, I was, once again, alone—not lonely, but alone. I found myself sitting at the edge of my bed, crying because she left but celebrating because she lived, all in the exact moment. My heart was heavy, yet still I rejoiced.

I learned the art of forgiveness through this moment. True forgiveness is found in our ability to release. With every release, we stand to gain something even when it doesn't feel like it. Trust me. It doesn't always feel good. We have to trust the process. When we seemingly lose a lot or have been hurt often, we tend to want to hold on to the pain. At that point, it has become a crutch. I believe that we hold on because, to some degree, we enjoy what comes with it. There are times where we become accustomed to the attention that it brings. We begin to desire to be appeased by the people around us. The sympathy that a down moment can get from the outside world becomes so soothing. In some strange way, it becomes our tunnel vision. We begin to thirst for affection. People will tell you that they want to heal from the pain of their past, yet their actions show different. We often scream to the rooftops that we are whole and try our best to put that wholeness on display to the world, especially in modern times. It's so easy for us to display it through social media. Showing people only what we want them to see—giving everyone the glitz and glam encounters of our lives. Trust me, there's nothing wrong with sharing good moments and being private to a certain degree. We face the problem in the motives behind what we share— masking our broken moments but criticizing and judging others in theirs.

I have stood the ultimate test of forgiving , having heard the things said about me behind my back and having those same people smile in my face and become upset because I refuse to continue living in the toxin-filled environments of their opinions or their theories about who you are or should be.

When we heal, we also allow those around us and those we encounter to do the same. The first sign of a lack of wholeness is in an individual's consistent action of judging others. Where the person constantly downplays the path of those they claim to love. When we are whole, we are thriving. We are focused on the things that will make us better. We begin pouring our time and attention into personal growth and building a better world around us. We become excited about the success of others. We can support and build them up with no thought of what we can gain from it. In doing so, we will have a head-on collision with 'true' forgiveness.

You see, it starts with you. You have to be willing to be brutally honest with the person that lies beneath the surface. Open heart surgery has to be performed so you can get to the deep-seated places of your intentions, the place where you are willing to experience real growth that welcomes and resonates with you becoming better in every aspect of your life.

You have to take a seat at the evaluation table and pick apart everyone and everything around you. The most extraordinary power you will ever possess is the ability to let go of people and things that no longer serve a purpose in your life all while being willing to accept and understand that it doesn't mean that those people and things hold no value. It's just they can no longer give you what you need in this season. That's ok! The walk of forgiveness has to be run like a business. You have to pull out a list and make a column for assets versus liabilities. Assets build, push, encourage, protect, respect, and value every aspect of you while liabilities judge, cripple, discourage and suck the life out of you. Liabilities are tricky. They come wrapped in a bow at times with excellent packaging. They tend to be compiled of all the things you seem to need. The truth is, during your "places of distraction," they may have been what you needed. Just know those needs are based on your perception at the time.

If you never grab hold of anything else in the world, you must know and understand you have to learn the art of genuine forgiveness. You have to begin first with forgiving yourself and acknowledge that we all fall short and make mistakes. It doesn't make you any less called or qualified for your purpose. If anything, it will equip you even more when you begin nurturing yourself and feeding your inner man first. Make that a number one priority in your life. It will take root and start leaving less room for empty moments. When you love and forgive yourself to the degree that supersedes human comprehension, it won't matter what anyone says. You'll no longer allow anyone or situation to put you in a box. You'll begin bursting at the seams, exuding all of the things you need to have the life you desire.

You'll spend less time chasing anything that doesn't feed you. You will refuse to entertain anyone that isn't pouring into you. You will become your most sacred and most prized possession. You will begin to love yourself like none other. It's then that you will have the power to manifest the atmosphere around you to pave the way to where you desire to be. Anything that doesn't line up with the destination will become uncomfortable in your presence.

Decide to become whole in no longer allowing your places of discomfort to be a place where you become comfortable. Don't you dare, for one minute, turn around to feed their superficial egos? Allow them to be who they are, understanding that they are no longer what you need. Become one with the fact that you have finally had a real encounter with peace that passes all understanding and that you have genuinely become whole. You found true forgiveness in your ability to forgive yourself.

Reflections

1. How do you define forgiveness?
2. In what areas of your life do you need to forgive yourself?
3. What are the situations in your life that need your forgiveness?
4. What actions have you taken towards that area of forgiveness?
5. How hard has submitting to that forgiveness been for you?

ACCEPTANCE

"The action of consenting to receive or undertake something offered"

"It is not the strongest or the most intelligent who will survive but those who can best manage change."

— Charles Darwin

S ometimes the hardest thing for us to do is accept where we are and what we have gone through. It can become overwhelming because it makes every obstacle and decision seem final.

"At the point of acceptance, we tend to believe that there is no longer room for change." — **Mel Jackson.**

As we grow, we will all experience things in life, including some that don't always make us proud. Often we experience things so ugly and disheartening that we want to forget. Of course, there is a pain that comes with reliving the inevitable, but there can also be a sense of peace if we embrace our shortcomings for the same amount of pain. When we begin to accept that every situation is the stepping stone to a greater you, we can find peace. Every encounter is an added piece to the puzzle. "The race is not given to the swift" (Ecclesiastes 9:11).

While finishing this book, I experienced some trials that I couldn't see my way out through. It was so heavy, I almost quit. Everything in that moment told me I wasn't qualified or equipped to complete the process. When I had my zoom meeting with the publisher to finalize the contract, she spoke a word over my life that encouraged me from a different place. After signing the contract, she said, "Mel, God wants you to know, everything you have gone through was to stop you from this moment!"

Not knowing what I was going through and having no clue that I had considered not going forth with the project, I felt the timing wasn't right for a minute. I have held on to those words. Boy, let me tell you something, though. It's something about the PUSH! It's something about standing in the face of adversity and declaring, "I WILL STILL WIN!" It's something about the anointing of God that will make you keep moving even when you want to quit. Even when you can't see a way or a light at the end of the tunnel, don't stop moving.

As I write to you, I am writing in a broken moment. We have to understand our career elevations, affiliations, social circle, monetary success, etc., will never exempt us from broken moments. Yes, I said broken *moments*, not *places*. When you learn the art of acceptance, it will shift your thoughts, and if your thoughts shift, you have to shift your language.

A place by definition is, a portion of space available or designated for or being used by someone. People tend to settle into places. However, a moment is a very brief period of time. When I started writing this book, I named it *Blessings in Broken Places*. I had settled in those places of distraction, and I had every intention of staying there. Let me be clear so you don't misunderstand what I'm conveying to you. Places are essential because they give birth to the moments. However, the only way that can be possible is if we learn to stop settling in the places of our distractions

We can no longer be stuck in a place of subconscious suffering, where you settle into a place and become comfortable. You have to stand up to yourself, speak to yourself and begin to encourage yourself. In the days leading up to finishing this project, my emotions were heavy. I felt defeated and alone. I would lay in bed and cry. As I looked over my life and my current situation, I asked, "What now? How do I move forward?"

After a couple of days of back and forth with myself, I lit the candles on top of the cake for my pity party, blew them out, and cut a piece. I vowed to myself that it would be the last slice of cake baked with misery, shame, and discouragement I would ever eat. I got out of that bed and said I would put one foot in front of the other, and I'm going to walk. I refused to stop moving, I refused to stop living, and I refused to stop trusting God. As I write this, I couldn't do it to my ability. I had to go into a place of prayer that produced a real encounter with perseverance, one that had experience and that my spirit could resonate with. I needed a divine encounter. I had a date with myself that was a dress rehearsal for my destiny.

I sat down at the table with my purpose, and I refused to get up until I could see the fruit of my labor pains. I was giving birth to this baby. In this season - "Come Hell or High Water." Most women can attest to the fact that being pregnant is exhausting in the last trimester. Yet, there is something about determination. Everything that I had encountered thus far had set the precedence for what I was now walking. I refused to allow all of the broken places of my past to overshadow this broken moment. Instead, I accepted the places in which I had been. I understood all of the distractions that accompanied those places had been a preview of the moment to come.

You see, at that moment, I found absolute joy and genuine peace. I found comfort that didn't come from people, and I discovered something extraordinary. I found myself, the self that had laid dormant behind all of the hurt and frustration, the self that had begun to understand and accept the abuse, abandonment, pain, and loss. The person inside that had become one with genuine love and forgiveness. I had shifted my perception and accepted ME!!!!

I packed my bags and moved from that place and began living in the moment. "Therefore, I tell you, do not worry about your life" (Matthew 6:25). In doing so, I realized that life is more than what you go through. It's more than merely existing. We have to distinguish the difference between places and moments in our lives. No matter how scared we are and the outcome, maybe we can never stop moving. Have you ever been faced with a situation and dreaded the result because all things considered, you couldn't see a way out? Sitting and looking at all of the facts involved, you were forced to believe that it could never work in your favor? Rest assured that it's designed to make you think like that when you are in this place.

Some aspire to provide hope to those who will lend an ear to hear and will look back over their life and tell all about what they've gone through and how they made it out, yet they are unwilling to share the trials of their present moment. We often take this approach because we are still living in these places. We tend to tread very lightly when declaring our faith that we will come out of the obstacle versus sharing the situations we've already overcome. These actions usually are rooted and grounded in being overly concerned with the opinions of others. Having this thought process leads one to ask, "How will they view us if what we speak, as the result of distractions, never manifests?"

It is then where we will have to decide whether we will settle in that place or live in the moment. You have to dig deep and come to the realization and be honest with yourself about where you truly desire to be. While walking through this moment, I desired to be sure that it didn't become my permanent place of residence.

I had settled into many places in my past, had picked out the furniture, and made them all warm and cozy because I was comfortable there. Why? You see, my places of distraction had become familiar to me. They were my safe zones. If I could hold on to them, I was protected from being vulnerable. I could relate to the baggage that I carried around from these places to the point where I felt I needed them because without them, I would feel empty. They had begun to define me. They had taken control of my thinking and my emotions. If I am frank, they began taking over my life. They made me skeptical of every situation and everyone. I had become initialized by distraction. It was easier to live in my distractions versus living through them.

The abuse had become the vehicle, and abandonment had become my driver. The loss had become the destination, and pain had become my best friend. I needed a new path to travel. I was looking for a different route to take. I was criticized by perception, victimized by love, and crippled by my inability to understand real forgiveness. Not knowing the day I made a solid decision to finish this book, acceptance would become my one-way ticket out of everything that held me captive for so long. It would become a breath of fresh air for me. It would change my perception and allow me to finally close the door on all of the things that I thought I needed.

I hope that you will heal, just as I have recovered. My prayer is that you will live in the moment of acceptance. What I desire more than anything, not only for myself but for the world that lives in the place of misguided, life distractions, is for us all to understand that the "distracted place" should guide us, not hinder us. If you can begin to see those places differently, you can accomplish and overcome anything.

Don't settle into a place and succumb to the bullying for the little girl who has been bullied. To the boy who has been mistreated, you shall overcome your hurt. For the woman who has been victimized or abused, know this is not who you were designed to be. These things may have happened to you but are not who you are. For the man who feels he has been emasculated, rise above that voice that says you're never going to be good enough.

Begin rebuilding in your moments. Be gracious and kind to yourself. The best version of you comes from what you say to yourself daily. It comes from the image of who stares back at you when you look in the mirror. *Mask off* in every situation. Get down to the core of your distractions and wrestle with them until you can see how they have equipped you for where you're going. You have to refuse to let go until actual results are produced. No longer accept band-aid results in uncomfortable places. Understand that hiding behind what happened to you isn't going to change the fact that it happened.

The path from distractions to acceptance is not easily traveled. Along the way, you will face many delays and disruption and unimaginable setbacks. Everyone wants the result, yet no one wants to go through the fire. For years, I have put my life on display to people I trusted. I told them some of my deepest secrets and allowed them to witness some of my darkest moments. Some of those times occurred beyond my control. I have been betrayed, lied to, talked about, and suffered from the wrong perception of me by others. In those moments, I prayed and cried while crying and praying. I could not understand how people could do these things to me. How could my actions and intentions be so often misunderstood? Why was it that at every turn, it seemed as though those closest to me were waiting for me to slip up, so they could use it against me?

In this season of my life, as I conclude this book, I am living that hurt. I am living that pain. I have sat in the quietest places alone, the areas where I could no longer refuse not to feel to receive my ultimate healing and have a clear vision. I could begin to understand that those who doubted my call and my ability to rise above really only doubted their ability to do so—understanding that when people can't see past their distractions, they will try to hold you hostage in yours.

I have yielded to my moment and have declared I will rise above the status quo of opinions. I learned to drown out the noise of the naysayers. I realized that there would always be something or someone that contradicted my destination. There would constantly be stumbling blocks. Knowing the only way one will ever survive is if you are bold enough to take the mask off in the moment if you have enough courage to tell people about your broken places. Show them who you are based on the facts of your life versus the bits and pieces they may have heard from others, in an attempt to define your moment or distort their vision of you. Take back the opinion of society that says you would continuously operate from your places.

Today, I urge you to close the door, pack your bags, and call the movers. Today I encourage you to live in the moment you deserve.

Reflections

1. What does acceptance mean to you?
2. What emotions do you feel when faced with a decision to accept your life distractions?
3. What places in your life have you adapted to versus the moments in which you have lived?
4. How do you feel the "places" in your life helped develop your growth?
5. What does "living in the moment" mean to you?

Mel Jackson

UNMASK CHALLENGE

A s you read through this book, I have shared with you my broken places, giving you all of the jewels and inspiration of how I navigated from one broken place to the next. Now, I challenge you to take all that you have learned and begin to unmask. First, take some time to sit quietly and reflect on your life. Then, using the butterfly mask design on the following page as a visual, what are the areas of your life where you can begin unmasking? Find a place where you can become completely vulnerable and transparent and no longer be afraid to share these areas for fear of judgment, somewhere where you can begin to embark upon your journey to acceptance in the purest form.

Love,
Mel J.

Mel Jackson

REFERENCES

1. Luke. "The Art of Forgiveness." Mindview Psychology, April 16, 2019. https://mindviewpsychology.com.au/the-art-of-for-giveness/.

2. Holy Bible, New International Version®, NIV® Copyright ©1973, 1978, 1984, 2011 by Biblica, Inc.® Used by permission. All rights reserved worldwide.

3. *The Bible.* Authorized King James Version, Oxford UP, 1998.

4. "place." *Merriam-Webster.com.* 2021. https://www.merriam-webster.com (2 July 2021).

5. "moment." *Merriam-Webster.com.* 2021. https://www.merriam-webster.com (2 July 2021).

Made in the USA
Monee, IL
18 November 2021

82409309R10066